Writing Prompts For Depression and Anxiety

A 100 Day Journal To Ease Depression And Anxiety

By

Subha Malik

Writing Prompts For Depression and Anxiety

A 100 Day Journal To Ease Depression And Anxiety

Author: SUBHA MALIK

Printed in the United States of America

1st printing [October/2018]

ISBN-13: 978-1729551837
ISBN-10: 1729551831

Introduction:

"Writing Prompts for Depression And Anxiety" is a 100-day journal to help you ease your depression and anxiety. It comes with 101 well-thought-out journal prompts for individuals suffering from any stage of anxiety or depression.

There are many benefits of journaling or writing as it helps you to explore and discover your best version, it helps you slow down and increase self-awareness. Journaling is specifically important for depression and anxiety.

According to psychologist Barbara Markway;

"There's simply no better way to learn about your thought processes than to write them down."

According to positivepsychologyprogram.com, "Journaling can also help people suffering from anxiety disorders. Like depression, the positive outcomes are well-documented for this purpose. In fact, compared to many other aims when journaling, it is extremely well-suited to helping you deal with anxiety.

So, keeping in view the benefits and importance of journaling for self-help, I have crafted this self-help journal to help people with depression and anxiety.

The questions and writing prompts within this unique journal are meant to make you slow-down, watch your thoughts and pour them out on the paper. This journal will help you to dig deeper inside your depression and anxiety and help you think about some possible coping strategies to over stress, anxiety, and depression.

I am sure "Writing Prompts For Depression And Anxiety" will provide you with helpful things to write about.

Enjoy!

DEDICATION

This Book Is Dedicated to All the courageous people who are fighting with depression or anxiety and trying to kick it out. I also dedicate this effort to My Parents, My Beloved Wife, and My Three Little Angels!

ACKNOWLEDGMENTS

I would like to express my gratitude to all the wonderful people who played a vital role throughout my life like my parents, my teachers, my mentors, and my friends. I would not be able to create this Book and many others without their loyal support.

Especially I would like to thank my wife and the rest of my family, who supported and encourage me despite not giving them enough time.

ABOUT THE AUTHOR

Subha Malik is a blogger, writer, and author, he loves to write about self-help topics and his aim is to inspire people and help them live better lives.

You can check out his other books here:

amazon.com/author/subhamalik

Visit His Blog: www.positiveblaze.com

Let's dive in...

Write down 5 of your greatest qualities

Make a list of things you are grateful for

Write down your biggest challenges you are facing right now

On a scale of 1 to 10, my happiness level is _____ because...

Write about some of the really tough times you have managed to overcome

Write down 10 things that make you smile

Write about your evening routine. Also, write about things you can adjust in your evening routine to feel happier

Make a list of things you need to let go of

If you can travel anywhere in the world, where would you love to go? Why?

What is your patience level with others on a scale of 1-10?

Write about a time when you felt really embarrassed

Recall a time or situation when you helped someone. How did you feel?

The biggest lesson I have learned so far is...

Write down three of your long-term goals

Draw something that makes you happy

Describe your drawing as well

10 things that you love about life

What keeps you moving even when things seem tough?

What is something you have managed to kick out of your life for good?

10 things you do to take care of your physical or emotional health

Tell me about your achievements this month so far

Imagine a life without anxiety or depression. How would you feel and what things you would be able to do then?

How is your day going? Is it a difficult day? If yes, what made it a difficult day and what can you do to stop such difficult days in the future?

Write about a problem you have recently found a solution to. What did you do to overcome that problem?

Do you take a day off to relax and allow yourself to breathe? Why or why not?

Write a letter to your inner critic. Tell her about the things that she doesn't know about you

Write about every single positive change you have experienced during the past month

Write about the words you like or need to hear from others

I would like to be remembered for...

Every day I look forward to...

10 things you love to do when you aren't feeling depressed or anxious

Make a list of words that make you feel sad

Make a list of words or affirmations that lift your mood up

Recall your most pleasant memory and recall your feelings at that time

What are 5 things that trigger your anxiety or depression? Also, write about coping strategies you can use for each of the triggers

Revisit your past and write about things that you can forgive others for

Make a list of things you want to achieve
during next 5, 10 and 20 years

What are your biggest fears? Why do they make you so frightened?

Write about 5 moments when you were extremely happy

How do you want to start your day? And how would your perfect morning routine look like?

If you are feeling anxious or stressed, think about the possible ways you can adapt to revert to your normal condition

What are some easy peasy self-care activities you can do right now?

Do you think self-care is important for easing your anxiety or depression? Why or why not?

How can you move to the next level of life?
What skills can you improve upon to push
yourself to the next level of life

What is your story? What are things you keep telling yourself again and again about you, your capabilities and your future?

Rephrase your story by replacing the pessimistic thoughts with positive ones

How do you feel after rephrasing your story?

Write down everything that comes to your mind no matter how random it is

Right now, I am feeling....

Write down all of your victories for this month no matter how small they are. Think about the ways to celebrate them

Write about something you habitually do that lifts your mood up

Write about a perfect day that is full of joy, excitement, and happiness. What can you do to make it a perfect day?

Make a list of things you can do to ease

your depression or anxiety

Write down 5 of your favorite inspirational quotes

Right now, I am thankful for...

What do you like your life to feel like?

5 things that inspire you to work towards your goals are:

Discuss 3 things you did wrong this year. Also, write the lessons you have learned from them

Write down the names of some stressful people in your inner circle. Also, write down some possible ways to deal with them

Imagine the worst that might happen tomorrow

Write down your most effective stress coping strategies that worked in the past

List three positive things that can happen today or tomorrow

List all the cool things about yourself. These can be your skills, your achievements, your capabilities, and your personality traits

Now write down the feelings you are having after writing these things about you. Do you feel better?

Write about one of your biggest supporters. Who is he/she? Write a thank you letter to him/her

Write about your biggest achievements so far. What personal qualities enabled you to make those achievements?

Describe the things you have learned from your depression or anxiety

If I were totally fearless I would...

Describe the things you can do to overcome your biggest fear in life

My happiest childhood memories are:

My saddest childhood memories are:

Imagine a life without depression, anxiety, and stress. Write down all the amazing things you can do then

The bad habits that lead me to feel more anxious are:

Describe a perfect day from your past that you would like to relive over and over again. What is so special about that day?

How do you introduce yourself to strangers? Can you rephrase your words or totally change them to make your intro more exciting and energized?

My biggest values in life are:

Describe something that others don't understand about you. How is it affecting your life in general?

List 3 of your biggest learning moments

3 Things I want to change about myself are:

My biggest failure taught me...

List all the things that bug you most. How can you avoid them?

I want to be remembered as...

List top 5 compliments you've received till date

Do you procrastinate on things? Does it make you feel more stressed?

Do you know getting things done can make you less anxious? List pending things that you can do today to feel less anxious or stressed

Write down things you would like to do on your last day on the earth

Write about the biggest motivator in your life. Write a thank you letter to him/her

List 5 things you can do this week to improve your mental health

Write down all the things that you are feeling worried about today

What makes you think that you're anxious or stressed. Describe both physical and mental symptoms of your anxiety or depression

When was the last time you felt extremely happy and what made you feel that way? Try to relive that moment

How do you define failure? Do you re-try after failing at something or simply quit?

List all the things which are not working for you right now

Write about the most important people in your life. Also, write about your relationship with those people

Make a list of all the things that are bugging you today

Describe one thing you wish to tell someone. What is that and to whom you want to say that?

Carefully listen to your inner critic. What does it say to you and how can you challenge her?

Have you ever tried to expand your comfort zone? Does it make you feel more anxious? Why or why not?

What are your core values? Does your life match those values? If not, then what small adjustments can you make to match your life with your core values?

Describe the ways in which you can help yourself face uncertainty

What is your favorite quote that makes you feel good? Why it makes you feel positive?

What are some unkind words that you say to yourself every day? What can you tell yourself instead?

Leave a Review

If you enjoyed this Book, please don't forget to leave a review about this Book on Amazon! This way others can enjoy this too!

I'm just a home-based author with NO "big marketing company" behind me, so I highly appreciate your review, and it only takes a minute to do.

To Submit a Review:

1. Just go to Amazon and under the BOOKS category, search this Book's title;

   [Writing Prompts For Depression And Anxiety: A 100 Day Journal To Ease Depression And Anxiety
   ] to get to the product detail page for this eBook on Amazon.

2. Click **Write a customer review** in the Customer Reviews section.

3. Click Submit.

Thank you in advance for submitting it!"

Resources For Ideas & Inspiration For This Book

http://powerfulmind.co/journaling-prompts/

http://www.newlifefoundation.com/th/20-journaling-prompts-mental-health-emotional-balance

https://aspiringquill.com/60-journal-writing-prompts-for-depression-and-anxiety/

http://www.discobumblebee.com/20-journal-prompts-for-anxiety-and-depression/

https://www.merakilane.com/journaling-for-depression-and-anxiety-33-journal-prompts-for-mental-health/

 https://www.radicaltransformationproject.com/journal-writing-posts-personal-growth/

https://aimhappy.com/journaling-prompts-stress-relief/

https://www.createwritenow.com/journal-writing-blog/10-quick-journal-prompts-to-calm-your-mind

https://sharonmartincounseling.com/journal-prompts-relieve-stress-anxiety-counseling-san-jose/

https://www.rose-minded.com/single-post/Mental-Health-Journal-Prompts-for-Stress-Relief

https://www.theodysseyonline.com/journal-prompts-anxiety

Manufactured by Amazon.ca
Bolton, ON

24363068R00067